Blk+
vegan

Blk + vegan

Full-Flavor, Protein-Packed Recipes from My Kitchen to Yours

Emani Corcran

creator of Blk and Vegan

PAGE STREET
PUBLISHING CO.

PAGE STREET
PUBLISHING CO.

First published in 2023 by

Page Street Publishing Co.

27 Congress Street, Suite 1511

Salem, MA 01970

www.pagestreetpublishing.com

Distributed by Macmillan, sales in Canada by The Canadian Manda Group.

27   26   25   24   23   1   2   3   4   5

ISBN-13: 978-1-64567-755-0

ISBN-10: 1-64567-755-9

Library of Congress Control Number: 2022946552

Cover and book design by Meg Baskis for Page Street Publishing Co.

Photography by Monika Normand

Printed and bound in the United States

Page Street Publishing protects our planet by donating to nonprofits like The Trustees, which focuses on local land conservation.

Dedication

To Traci Anne, your daughter
is now an author.

Contents

Introduction

Hello dear readers,

I want to start this book with gratitude. Thank you so much for purchasing my book of recipes that were created from my heart. By picking up this book you have made a little girl's dream come true!

Growing up, my relationship with food was always exploratory and unique. I had a big hate for eggs and a wild curiosity about flavors. I can still remember almost burning the house down because I was trying to fry biscuit dough to make homemade donuts and writing down milkshake recipes at my grandmother's home to save them for later. Not to mention the countless times I daydreamed during school hours about what I would go home and make for lunch that day. Food always meant creativity, joy and ultimately community. Each holiday you would find me standing in the ktichen, prepping and cooking and soaking up any bit of knowledge I could. I wanted to take this knowledge and test it on my own cooking, so I could bring those traditions into my own future family.

My relationship with food changed as I grew up and experienced a grave amount of loss. My family, who traditionally ate meat as their main source of protein, was continuously sick. As the years went by, I wanted a way to change my family's narrative. I began to pursue a passion for health and fitness but I never equated health with a particular dietary choice. That all changed when I watched the *What the Health* documentary. For those that have never seen the documentary, it details the facts about plant-based diets, their nutritional value and their relationship to the meat industry. I learned that plants, legumes and fruits were placed on this Earth to heal us. A lightbulb went off in my head and within a short time span, I decided to dedicate my life to veganism. I started my food blog Blk and Vegan and began to share my vegan journey through cook-alongs and meat-eater-friendly recipes. Through sharing my journey, I gained a following and a place of refuge. My page has become a community of people banding together to discover plant-based meals at any stage of their journey. This book is an extension of that page and passion.

Coincidentally, I never thought the day would come that I would be the author of a cookbook, but looking back it's always been *food*: the vessel that brought people together, the smell that would make me run from my bedroom on Saturday morning and the cure I was continuously seeking. Within this book, you will find a mix of personal stories that describe my food journey. Each recipe was specifically chosen from a moment in my life or memory, such as the Southern-Style Greens (page 89) recipe that reminds me of my aunt's collards, the Heart of Palm Ceviche (page 93) I served at my sister's graduation party and the Easy Coffee Ice Cream (page 139) that reminds me of my mother. Everything in this book is crafted for the everyday home cook just like me, who loves flavor, texture and spices.

This book is dedicated to my mother, Traci, who never got the chance to try my vegan creations but inspired, guided and prepared me for this moment.

Welcome to my food diary.

Love, Emani

smoothies, milks and juices, oh my!

This is the section that is the start of my journey with you all. It's an awesome reflection of the first time I made vegan milk, shown in my 5-Minute Oat Milk (page 14) recipe, or the summer I spent focused on health and creating things that reflect that desire, exemplified in my Golden Milk (page 17) and Immune-Boosting Juice Blend (page 18) recipes. This chapter has recipes that are perfect for a single serving or a group, in particular the Spicy Lemon Tonic (page 26). I hope you love these recipes as much as I do.

5-minute oat milk

Serves: 4-6

This oat milk is so creamy—and so easy to make! When I first became vegan, I thought it was essential to learn how to make your own milk at least once. This recipe makes it easy and it is absolutely delicious, not to mention cheaper and fresher than anything you will find at the store.

1 cup (161 g) steel-cut oats
4 cups (960 ml) water
2 dates
1 tbsp (15 ml) vanilla
Pinch of salt

Cover a large bowl with one or two layers of cheesecloth and fasten the cheesecloth with a rubber band to make sure it stays on. Have another bowl and layer of cheesecloth on hand.

Add the oats, water, dates, vanilla and a pinch of salt to a high-speed blender and blend for 20 to 30 seconds. Drain the oat milk through the cheesecloth into the bowl. Remove the cheesecloth, and gently squeeze it to release excess moisture into the bowl. Throw away the excess oat solids. Put the extra layer of fresh cheesecloth on another bowl or container and repeat the draining and squeezing steps. Store the oat milk in an airtight container in the refrigerator for up to 4 days.

golden milk

 Serves: 1

This recipe is anti-inflammatory, protein-packed and so creamy. It is fueled with hemp seeds and turmeric to give you all the good vibes. It is also absolutely delicious—like drinking a cinnamon roll for breakfast!

1½ cups (360 ml) vegan milk of choice

3 tbsp (30 g) hemp seeds

1 tsp coconut oil

1 tsp vanilla

1 tbsp (14 g) brown sugar

1 tsp pre-minced ginger

1½ tsp (3 g) turmeric

½ tsp cinnamon

Fresh-cracked black pepper

Add the vegan milk, hemp seeds, coconut oil, vanilla, brown sugar, ginger, turmeric, cinnamon and a pinch of freshly cracked black pepper to a blender and blend until smooth, 3 to 5 minutes.

Add to a glass and enjoy!

pro tip: If you would like to make this hot, warm it in a sauce-pan over medium heat on the stove, or microwave for 1 minute and 30 seconds.

immune-boosting juice blend

Serves: 1

This juice blend is specifically formulated to boost your immunity, before you even know you need a boost! Packed with pineapple, coconut water and cucumber, it is super hydrating, as well as filled with vitamins and minerals to keep you feeling your best!

1 small cucumber

1 cup (165 g) pineapple chunks

Juice from ½ lemon

1 tbsp (15 g) pre-minced ginger

Sprinkle of cayenne

Large handful of spinach

2–3 cups (480–720 ml) coconut water, to taste

Combine the cucumber, pineapple, lemon juice, ginger, cayenne, spinach and coconut water in a blender along with ice, if desired. Blend for 2 minutes. Pour into a glass or jar and enjoy.

pro tip: If you don't want pulp in your juice, before pouring it into a glass or mason jar, cover the top of the glass or jar with a piece of cheesecloth. Secure the cheesecloth with a rubber band, and slowly pour your immunity blend through the cheesecloth. Take the rubber band off the cheesecloth and squeeze any excess moisture out of the cheesecloth into the glass or jar. Throw away the pulp and enjoy the juice immediately or store overnight in an airtight container in the refrigerator.

peanut butter and jelly smoothie

 Serves: 1

As a child I loved PB&Js, and even as an adult, I love to find ways to sneak them into my diet—why not in a delicious, nutritious smoothie? Most people are apprehensive about adding vegetables to smoothies, but trust me: The more veggies, the better. Especially when you can't taste them! That's why I love adding cauliflower to my smoothies–it has great nutrients with no taste and helps to create a luscious texture!

½ cup (74 g) blueberries

½ cup (60 g) minced frozen cauliflower

½ frozen banana

¼ cup (23 g) rolled oats

1 tbsp (16 g) peanut butter

1 tbsp (10 g) flax seeds

1 cup (240 ml) vegan milk of choice

1–2 scoops (3–6 tbsp [19–37 g]) vanilla protein powder of choice

½ cup ice

Add the blueberries, cauliflower, banana, oats, peanut butter, flax seeds, vegan milk, protein powder and ice to a high-speed blender and blend until deliciously creamy and smooth, around 2 minutes. Add to a glass or mason jar and enjoy.

pro tip: I love to prep my smoothie ingredients (excluding the vegan milk) and add them to a ziptop bag and store in the freezer until ready to use. When ready to use, add milk, blend and enjoy!

peach cobbler smoothie

 Serves: 1

Peach cobbler is one of my favorite desserts and, surprise, one of my favorite smoothie flavors. This one has cauliflower, which is the perfect hidden vegetable! You won't believe how good this is for you and you will never even taste it.

¾ cup (95 g) frozen peaches

½ cup (60 g) frozen cauliflower

¼ cup (23 g) rolled oats

1–2 scoops (3–6 tbsp [19–37 g]) vanilla protein powder of choice (optional)

½ tsp cinnamon

1 tsp vanilla (optional)

1 cup (240 ml) 5-Minute Oat Milk (page 14; or other vegan milk of choice)

Add the peaches, cauliflower, oats, protein powder (if using), cinnamon, vanilla (if using) and oat milk to a high-speed blender and blend until smooth, 3 to 5 minutes. Pour into a glass or mason jar and enjoy!

elderberry–mint refresher

 Serves: 4

In the past couple of years, health and immunity have become focal points of conversation. To no surprise, there are so many things within nature that are natural healers—like elderberry! Not only is it known to boost immunity, it's the perfect pretty purple to awe any audience while secretly being good for you.

1 cup (145 g) blackberries

6 mint sprigs, plus more for garnish

2 tbsp (30 ml) elderberry syrup

2–3 limes, sliced

¼ cup (50 g) organic sugar or sweetener of choice

3–4 cups (650–865 g) ice

1 (33.8-oz [1-L]) bottle tonic water

Place the blackberries, mint, elderberry syrup and lime slices at the bottom of a small bowl. Using a muddler, gently mash until well combined. Add the mixture to a pitcher, along with the sugar and mix well to dissolve the sugar. Add the ice and tonic water, and top with extra mint if desired. Serve immediately.

spicy lemon tonic

 Serves: 4

This is the perfect drink for a spicy treat! I loved creating this recipe because it's so easy, refreshing and the perfect thing to bring to any girls' or guys' night. If you're feeling frisky, spike with your favorite alcohol!

6 lemons, juiced, or 1 cup (240 ml) lemon juice

¼ cup (50 g) organic sugar or sweetener of choice

1 jalapeño pepper, thinly sliced

1 lemon, thinly sliced, for garnish

1 (33.8-oz [1-L]) bottle tonic water

Add the lemon juice to a large pitcher, then add the sugar and mix until well combined. Add the jalapeño and lemon slices and top with the tonic water. Fill with ice to the brim if serving quickly, mix well and serve. If not serving instantly, omit ice until ready to serve to avoid watering down your tonic.

oats, scrambles and puddings

My life has evolved so that breakfast has become one of my favorite meals. As a child, I hated eggs! My sister, on the other hand, loved them. So most of our meals consisted of egg scrambles and omelets—things that I gladly opted out of. As a vegan, I began to explore breakfast in a different way. No longer was I held to the expectation that eggs were a necessity, in fact quite the opposite. In this chapter, I touch upon some awesome childhood recipes, like Favorite Spiced Waffles (page 37), I veganize eggs in my Signature Tofu Scramble (page 42) and I highlight new favorites that I gained on my vegan journey, like two kinds of chia seed pudding (page 38 and page 41).

From sweet to savory there is something for everyone in this chapter! You will be so shocked at how delicious a vegan's breakfast can be and how easy—from single meals to family style, I've got you covered.

bursting blueberry oat cake

 Serves: 1–2

Have you ever had cake for breakfast? Well, what about healthy cake for breakfast? Don't tell a soul, but these blueberry baked oats are everything you are looking for in a satisfying breakfast. Toddlers to adults love this recipe because it's absolutely delicious! The oat base has a cake consistency and the blueberries add the perfect touch of sweetness. Say goodbye to mushy oats, and hello to your new obsession!

1 tsp oil of choice

1 whole ripe banana

1 cup (90 g) rolled oats

2 tsp (9 g) baking powder

¾ cup (180 ml) vegan milk

¼ tsp cinnamon (optional)

1 tsp vanilla

¼ cup (37 g) frozen blueberries (the berries sweeten it; if not using berries, add 1 tsp sweetener of choice)

Preheat the oven to 400°F (205°C). Use the oil to grease a 14-ounce (414-ml) oven-safe dish.

Add the banana, oats, baking powder, vegan milk, cinnamon (if using) and vanilla to a blender and blend for 3 minutes, until smooth. Add the oat mixture to the greased dish then add the frozen berries and mix. Bake for 32 to 35 minutes, until a toothpick comes out clean.

apple-spiced oat cake

Serves: 1–2

These baked oats are like having a warm cinnamon cake, but for breakfast! They are so good, but most importantly, they lower inflammation and blood sugar and ease weight loss. Move aside mushy oats, there is a new flavorful sidekick in town that just may steal the show.

1 tsp oil of choice

⅔ cup (160 ml) vegan yogurt (or 1 banana)

1 cup (90 g) rolled oats

¾ cup (180 ml) vegan milk

2 tsp (9 g) baking powder

1 tsp vanilla

1 cup (120 g) diced apples

1 tbsp (15 ml) maple syrup

1 tsp turmeric

1 tsp cinnamon

1 tsp ginger

Pinch of pepper (to activate the turmeric)

Preheat the oven to 400°F (205°C). Use the oil to grease a 14-ounce (414-ml) oven-safe dish.

Add the yogurt (or banana), oats, vegan milk, baking powder and vanilla to a blender and blend for 3 minutes, until smooth. Add the oat mixture to the greased pan.

In a saucepan over medium–low heat, add 3 to 4 tablespoons (45–60 ml) of water along with the apples, maple syrup, turmeric, cinnamon, ginger and pepper and sauté until tender, 2 to 4 minutes. Add the spiced apple mixture to the oats and mix until combined. Bake for 32 to 35 minutes, until a toothpick comes out clean.

fluffy protein-packed pancakes

 Serves: 3-4

We all love pancakes. When I was younger, pancakes were definitely made on weekends when we were able to spend breakfast together as a family. During the week, we would always rush to school, work or errands, but the weekends were set for a huge family breakfast, and I always looked forward to pancakes. These pancakes in particular are guilt-free because they are packed with protein and so flavorful! Enjoy.

2 bananas, ripe

2 cups (480 ml) vegan milk

¾ cup (180 ml) water

1 tsp vanilla

4 tsp (18 g) baking powder

2 cups (240 g) whole-wheat flour

1 tsp salt

1 tsp cinnamon

2 tbsp (20 g) flax seeds

1–2 scoops (3–6 tbsp [19–37 g]) protein powder

Vegan butter or oil of choice

Combine the bananas, vegan milk, water, vanilla, baking powder, flour, salt, cinnamon, flax seeds and protein powder in a high-speed blender until nice and smooth, around 3 minutes. Set aside.

Add 1 teaspoon of butter or oil of choice to a pan or griddle warmed over medium–low heat. Pour about ¼ cup (60 ml) of batter per pancake into the pan. When the batter begins to bubble (this will take 3 to 4 minutes), flip the pancake and cook until the bottom is set. Top with whatever you like and enjoy!

favorite spiced waffles

 Serves: 4

Growing up, my aunt would make the absolute best spiced waffles. In my family, spiced waffles involve a ton of cinnamon and maybe even a clove or two. Waking up on Saturday morning and following the smell of cinnamon and vanilla to the kitchen was my absolute favorite part of the weekend. Here's my version of those delicious spiced waffles, made with love—oil-free and absolutely delicious.

2 tbsp (20 g) flax seeds

6 tbsp (90 ml) water

2 cups (240 g) whole-wheat flour

1 tbsp (14 g) baking powder

Heavy pinch salt

2 tbsp (28 g) brown sugar

½ tsp turmeric

Sprinkle black pepper

2 tsp (6 g) cinnamon

⅓ cup (80 g) applesauce

2 cups (480 ml) vegan milk

1 tbsp (15 ml) vanilla

Fresh fruit, for serving

Whipped cream, for serving

Maple syrup, for serving

In a small bowl, mix the flax seeds and water and let the mixture sit for 5 minutes.

To a medium bowl, add the flour, baking powder, salt, brown sugar, turmeric, black pepper and cinnamon and give it a good mix until well combined.

In another medium bowl, mix the applesauce, vegan milk, vanilla and flax seed mixture until well combined. Slowly add the dry ingredients to the wet ingredients about 1 cup (240 ml) at a time and gently mix until well combined.

Preheat a waffle iron, and if it is not non-stick, coat it with some oil to keep the waffle mix from sticking.

Pour ¾ to 1 cup (180–240 ml) of the waffle mix into the waffle iron and cook until heated through, 8 to 10 minutes (or when your waffle machine alerts you that the waffle is ready). Enjoy with fruit, whipped cream and maple syrup.

protein-packed chia seed pudding

 Serves: 4

If you're looking for that quick, meal prep-able breakfast that is packed with fiber, protein and antioxidants, this puppy is for you. It's so easy to whip together the night before a busy morning and its texture is similar to the tapioca pudding we used to have as kids. When I discovered how to make this, it was pretty much my go-to breakfast for weeks on end. The best tip when eating this dish is to choose a vegan protein powder that you enjoy!

½ cup (81 g) chia seeds

1–2 scoops (3–6 tbsp [19–37 g]) protein powder of choice

¾ tsp cinnamon

2–2½ cups (480–600 ml) vegan milk

2 tsp (10 ml) vanilla

Mixed fruit, for serving

Walnuts, for serving

Add the chia seeds, protein powder and cinnamon to a bowl and give it a good mix. Add the milk and vanilla and stir until combined. Refrigerate the mixture for 4 hours or allow to set overnight.

Top as desired. I prefer an assortment of fruits and walnuts.

mango coconut chia seed pudding

Serves: 4

Mango and coconut have my heart. Adding these flavors to a chia seed pudding just increased my love for a good chia seed pudding. This is super meal prep-able, not to mention the perfect breakfast to wake up to.

½ cup (85 g) mango, plus more for serving

1 cup (240 ml) sweetened coconut milk

½ cup (120 ml) water

1 tbsp (15 ml) maple syrup

1 tsp vanilla

½ cup (81 g) chia seeds, plus more for serving

Shredded coconut, for serving

Add the mango, coconut milk, water, maple syrup and vanilla to a high-speed blender and purée. Add the chia seeds to a medium-sized bowl, pour in the mango purée and give it a good mix. Cover the mixture with a paper towel or a lid. Refrigerate for 4 hours or allow to set overnight.

Serve with your favorite toppings—I like to top mine with extra mango, coconut shreds and chia seeds for texture.

signature tofu scramble

 Serves: 4

I hated eggs as a child. Hate is a strong word that I don't like to use often, so if I use it, you have to know that the dislike was real! Not surprisingly, when turning vegan, I was afraid of tofu. Would it taste just like eggs? Well, the answer is no! My favorite part about tofu is the fact that I can flavor it how I desire. So, let me introduce you to the scramble that made me love tofu.

1 cup (240 ml) vegetable stock or vegan chicken-less stock

½ yellow or red onion, diced

1 (14-oz [397-g]) package extra-firm tofu

¼ cup (11 g) nutritional yeast

2 tbsp (30 ml) soy sauce

2 tsp (4 g) curry powder

1 tsp garlic powder

1 tsp paprika

½ tsp onion powder

½ tsp smoked paprika (optional)

Add the stock and diced onion to a medium-sized pan over medium–high heat. Crumble the tofu into the pan. Add the nutritional yeast, soy sauce, curry powder, garlic powder, paprika, onion powder and smoked paprika (if using) and mix until combined. Cover the pan and turn down the heat to medium–low. Cook until the liquid is absorbed, 10 to 12 minutes, then enjoy!

vegan chilaquiles

 Serves: 4

This chilaquiles recipe is so easy to make and it's a crowd favorite. I make this when I am craving a savory breakfast. Traditionally this dish is served with eggs, but I make mine with tofu and it's absolutely delicious. This is the perfect meal to make for a slow morning at home!

7 oz (198 g) extra-firm tofu

1 small zucchini

½ red onion, diced

2 cups (60 g) spinach

4 cloves garlic, diced

¼ cup (11 g) nutritional yeast

2 tbsp (30 ml) soy sauce

3–4 tsp (7–9 g) salt-free Mexican seasoning

Salt and pepper, to taste

2 cups (480 ml) vegetable or vegan chicken-less broth

1 (12-oz [340-g]) bag stone-ground corn chips

1 cup (240 ml) enchilada sauce of choice

1 cup (260 g) pinto or black beans

½ cup (60 g) vegan fresco (or cheese of choice)

½ cup (120 ml) vegan sour cream

½ cup (120 ml) pico de gallo

Handful fresh cilantro

1 avocado, sliced

Preheat the oven to 400°F (205°C).

Drain the tofu and wrap it in two to three paper towels and gently press to remove excess moisture while you prepare the zucchini. Grate the zucchini into an unheated pot. Grate the tofu into the same pot, then add the onion, spinach, garlic, nutritional yeast, soy sauce, Mexican seasoning, salt and pepper and broth. Place the pot on medium–low heat and cook until all the liquid is absorbed, stirring occasionally (this will take about 25 minutes).

Meanwhile, when the oven is preheated, add the chips to a 9 x 13–inch (23 x 33–cm) baking dish, spray them with some avocado oil and place in the oven for 5 minutes to crisp.

When the chips and tofu mixture are ready, top the chips with the enchilada sauce, beans and the tofu mixture. Garnish with vegan fresco, vegan sour cream, pico de gallo, cilantro and avocado.

pasta and rice for the soul

Growing up, spaghetti was a staple. Much like greens, everyone has their own way of making their spaghetti. As a child, I would love any table I was at that served a giant bowl of it. As I am writing this, I can still remember the taste of my grandmother's spaghetti versus the healthy carrot-infused version my mom would make. That's what may have begun my love for pasta, and it is reflected in dishes like my Spicy Lentil Bolognese (page 52) and the Creamy Alfredo (page 51).

I started making rice dishes as I got older. I was always intimidated that I would cook rice incorrectly so I stayed far away. It wasn't until I met my now partner that I was inspired to see rice in a different way. It's not scary, boring or bland. It's a playground to infuse with flavor and prefers to be left alone while cooking, unattended, to do its thing. You can find the dish where I learned to fall in love with rice in this chapter; spoiler alert—it's the Caribbean Rice and Beans (page 60)!

Truthfully, you can never go wrong with a delicious bowl of pasta or a hearty bowl of rice.

chinese "chick"n salad pasta

Serves: 4

Say hello to the perfect meal prep! I took a fun spin on the classic Chinese Chicken Salad and made it one better by adding some pasta! This is the perfect chilled pasta that can turn any vegan skeptic into a fan. Perfect for a gathering, it brings a different flavor profile than your traditional pasta salad. Not to mention it's secretly packed with vegan protein—but don't tell anyone, it's between me and you!

8 oz (226 g) whole-wheat spaghetti

½ large Napa cabbage

11 oz (312 g) extra-firm tofu, sliced into thick slices

½ cup (46 g) edamame

¾ cup (142 g) mandarin oranges

½ cup (55 g) shredded carrot

2 large green onions, chopped

Large handful cilantro, plus more for garnish

5 mini cucumbers, chopped

½ cup (73 g) roasted unsalted peanuts, plus more for garnish

¼ cup (60 ml) soy sauce

¼ cup (60 ml) rice wine vinegar

2 tbsp (30 ml) sesame oil

1 mandarin, juiced

½ tbsp (7 g) minced fresh ginger

2 cloves garlic, minced

Red chili flakes (optional)

Cook the whole-wheat spaghetti according to the directions on the package.

Heat a grill or grill pan to a medium–high heat, coat with a layer of oil and place the Napa cabbage and tofu slices on the grill. Cook until you get a nice char, 5 to 7 minutes, flipping halfway through.

Chop the grilled cabbage and place it in a large serving bowl, along with the cooked pasta, edamame, oranges, carrots, green onions, cilantro, cucumbers and peanuts. Set aside.

Add the soy sauce, rice wine vinegar, sesame oil, orange juice, ginger, garlic and red chili flakes (if using) to a small bowl and whisk until combined.

Top the pasta salad with the dressing, give it a good mix and top with the grilled tofu, extra peanuts and cilantro.

creamy alfredo

 Serves: 4

This alfredo recipe is so creamy and delicious, not to mention packed with protein! When I was younger, fettuccini alfredo was my favorite thing to order at a restaurant—with extra cheese! Times have changed but one thing remains the same, alfredo is meant to be creamy and luscious! This vegan version does not disappoint.

1 cup (146 g) cashews

5–7 cloves garlic

12 oz (340 g) noodles of choice

1 (14-oz [397-g]) package silken tofu

1 cup (240 ml) vegan milk of choice

½ lemon, juiced

¼ cup (11 g) nutritional yeast

1 tbsp (5 g) dried basil

Salt and pepper, to taste

Crushed red chili flakes, to taste (optional)

Fresh basil, for garnish

Add the cashews, garlic cloves, and 8 cups (1.9 L) of water to a medium pot, bring to a boil and cook until the cashews and garlic cloves are tender, about 20 minutes. Drain.

Cook the noodles according to package directions and reserve ¼ cup (60 ml) of the cooking water before draining.

Add the drained garlic and cashews to a high-speed blender along with the silken tofu, vegan milk, lemon juice, nutritional yeast, dried basil and a generous amount of salt and pepper. Blend until smooth, about 5 minutes.

Add the cooked noodles, the reserved ¼ cup (60 ml) of pasta water and the cream mixture to a pot or serving bowl and mix until well combined. Garnish with crushed red chili flakes (if using), fresh basil or your toppings of choice.

spicy lentil bolognese

Serves: 2–3

Growing up, everyone in my family had their own way of making their spaghetti. My grandmother would keep things super simple and add a touch of sugar, whereas my mom would always add some carrots to hers for flair. However you make your spaghetti is up to you, but one thing is for sure: Going vegan doesn't mean you need to alter the flavor, protein or savoriness of your favorite spaghetti. The recipe below combines some fresh herbs for flavor, lentils for protein and walnuts for texture. Enjoy!

1 tsp dried basil

1 tsp red chili flakes

1 tsp paprika

1 tsp coriander

½ tsp turmeric

¼ tsp mustard powder (activates nutrients in veggies)

Salt and pepper, to taste

8 oz (226 g) spaghetti

1 tbsp (15 ml) oil of choice

2–3 cloves garlic, minced

¼ cup (40 g) chopped red onion

¼ cup (29 g) chopped walnuts

1 cup (240 ml) favorite tomato-based pasta sauce

1 cup (198 g) cooked lentils

Handful fresh basil

1 tbsp (10 g) flax seeds (optional)

1 tbsp (3 g) nutritional yeast (optional)

Handful spinach (optional)

Add the dried basil, chili flakes, paprika, coriander, turmeric, mustard powder, and salt and pepper to a small bowl, stir to combine, then set aside.

Cook the pasta according to package directions and reserve ½ to ⅔ cup (120–180 ml) of the cooking water before draining.

Add the oil to a medium-sized saucepan over medium heat, then add the garlic, onion and walnuts. Sauté for 2 to 3 minutes. Add the seasoning blend and stir to combine. Top with the tomato sauce, reserved pasta water and lentils. Cover, reduce the heat to low and simmer for 5 minutes. Place the cooked spaghetti in individual serving bowls, then top with the sauce and the fresh basil. Finish the dish with flax seeds, nutritional yeast and spinach, if desired.

creamy vodka pasta

 Serves: 2-3

Remember when the Internet went crazy for vodka pasta? Of course I had to take my stab at it! If you missed it, there was a long phase when vodka pasta was trending on social media. I could not go a day without seeing someone talking about, re-creating or posting this pasta. Surprisingly, going vegan doesn't mean you have to alter this recipe's amazing creaminess and taste. My vodka pasta recipe is made with creamy cashews for silkiness and a ton of garlic for flavor! Don't forget to add some nutritional yeast to bring that cheesy flavor we all know and love. Enjoy!

½ cup (73 g) cashews

1 cup (240 ml) vegan milk of choice

8 oz (226 g) pasta of choice

2 tbsp (30 ml) oil of choice

½ red onion or shallot, minced

6 cloves garlic, minced

1 tsp red chili flakes

6 tbsp (96 g) tomato paste

2 tbsp (32 g) sun-dried tomato paste (sub tomato paste if needed)

4 oz (120 ml) vodka of choice

1 tbsp (3 g) nutritional yeast (can sub with vegan cheese of choice)

Salt and pepper, to taste

Fresh basil, for garnish

Add the cashews to a pot of boiling water and cook on high heat for 15 minutes. Drain, then add to a blender along with the vegan milk. Blend until smooth, about 3 minutes, then set aside.

Prepare the pasta according to package directions in a large pot and reserve 1 cup (240 ml) of the water before draining.

In a saucepan, heat the oil on medium heat for around 3 minutes, then add the onion, garlic and red chili flakes. Sauté until fragrant, about 5 minutes. Add the tomato paste and sun-dried tomato paste, and mix until well combined. Next, add the vodka and simmer for 3 minutes. Add the reserved pasta water, cashew cream, nutritional yeast, and salt and pepper. Toss in your pasta, top with basil and enjoy!

a vegan's mac and cheese

 Serves: 4

I know, making mac and cheese as a vegan can be scary . . . even daunting. Well, no need to fear, I am here and will guide you to making the most creamy, flavorful mac and cheese that is even better than that old stuff you used to eat. Why? Because it's just as creamy, flavorful and delicious all while being incredibly protein-packed! Let's get into the best vegan mac you've had so far.

1 whole head garlic

½ red bell pepper

Salt and pepper

Avocado oil, for drizzling

1 cup (146 g) cashews

1 cup (200 g) dried chickpeas

2½ cups (315 g) whole-wheat macaroni

2 cups (480 ml) vegan milk of choice

½ cup (22 g) nutritional yeast

½ lemon, juiced

¾ cup (184 g) pumpkin purée

½ yellow onion, minced

5 leaves fresh sage, chopped

1 tbsp (5 g) red chili flakes (optional)

1 tsp oil of choice

½ cup (120 ml) water

1 tbsp (15 ml) maple syrup

2 tsp (4 g) coriander

1 tsp garlic powder

1 tsp onion powder

¼ tsp turmeric

Preheat the oven to 400°F (205°C).

Slice off about one quarter of the top of the head of garlic. Add the red bell pepper and head of garlic to a sheet pan and top with salt, pepper and a drizzle of avocado oil. Bake for 25 minutes. Remove the red bell pepper and set aside, then return the garlic to the oven for an additional 10 to 15 minutes.

In the meantime, add the cashews and chickpeas to a pot of water and boil for 15 to 20 minutes on high. Drain.

Cook the macaroni according to package directions.

Now here comes the easy part! Add the boiled cashews and chickpeas, roasted garlic flesh (omitting skin), roasted bell pepper, vegan milk, nutritional yeast, lemon juice and pumpkin purée to a blender and blend until smooth.

Sauté the onion, chopped sage and red chili flakes (if using) over medium heat in a teaspoon of oil. When the onion is tender and fragrant, 3 to 4 minutes, add the creamy blended sauce, water, maple syrup, coriander, garlic powder, onion powder, turmeric, salt, pepper and noodles and mix. Enjoy your first bite of a successful vegan mac and cheese made by you.

classic jambalaya

 Serves: 4

There is nothing I loved more as a child than jambalaya! My aunt would make a super quick version using the pre-made spiced rice mix, and I fell in love every time. I mean, as a meat eater, who wouldn't love jambalaya? It's infused with flavor. Well, in thinking of making my own vegan version, I knew those Louisiana flavors were essential to bringing back those memories and creating new ones! Dig into the jambalaya that reminds me of what it was like to sit at the table with excitement and look forward to leftovers the next day!

1–2 tsp red chili flakes

2 tsp (9 g) Cajun seasoning

1 tsp onion powder

½ tsp sea moss seasoning (or nori)

1 tbsp (15 ml) oil of choice

½ yellow onion, diced

1 Roma tomato, diced

5 cloves garlic, diced

1 tbsp (16 g) tomato paste

1 cup (200 g) uncooked brown rice, washed

½ cup (75 g) chopped green and red bell pepper

¼ cup (39 g) fresh corn

⅓ cup (38 g) frozen sliced okra

½ stalk celery, diced

2 tbsp (8 g) chopped fresh parsley, plus more for topping

4 oz (113 g) tempeh, diced

⅓ cup (80 ml) tomato sauce

2½ cups (600 ml) water

1 bay leaf

In a small bowl, mix the chili flakes, Cajun seasoning, onion powder and sea moss seasoning. Set aside.

Add the oil, onion, tomato and garlic to a medium-large pan over medium heat and sauté for 2 minutes. Add the tomato paste and the seasoning blend and sauté until fragrant, approximately 3 minutes.

After you can smell the seasonings begin to infuse, add the brown rice, bell peppers, corn, okra, celery and parsley and stir until combined. Add the diced tempeh, tomato sauce, water and bay leaf and increase the heat to high. Bring to a boil for 4 minutes, then simmer on low until the rice is tender, about 30 minutes. Avoid overmixing to prevent mushy rice!

Once the rice is tender, add to a large serving dish. Top with fresh parsley and enjoy!

caribbean rice and beans

 Serves: 4

This rice and beans recipe has saved me many times. It's the one-pot shop that we are all looking for on those nights we just don't feel like cooking (let's be honest!). This is a recipe that allows you to pour everything in a pot and come out with a seriously flavorful dish that honestly makes you feel like you put some TLC into it. Not to mention your home will smell amazing! P.S., this is also infused with protein and nutrients!

2 tbsp (30 ml) avocado oil

½ yellow onion, minced

3 cloves garlic, minced

2 tsp (12 g) jerk seasoning

½ tsp Cajun seasoning

¼ tsp coriander

¼ tsp turmeric

Pepper, to taste

2 cups (360 g) long-grain rice

1 (15.5-oz [439-g]) can beans of choice

1 (13.5-oz [398-ml]) can full-fat coconut milk

2½ cups (600 ml) water

Heat the oil in a saucepan over medium heat, then add the onion and garlic and sauté until fragrant, 2 to 3 minutes. Add the jerk seasoning, Cajun seasoning, coriander, turmeric and pepper and stir to combine. Add the rice and beans. Combine until well mixed then add the coconut milk and water. Gently stir and lower the heat to medium low for 10 minutes and then low until the rice is tender, 30 to 35 minutes.

protein-packed beans and tofu

Within this section, you will discover the central component to almost all of my meals. These recipes provide a protein punch packed with flavor that you can place on top of rice, pasta or any other grain or veggie you desire. Don't be fooled, you may just eat these dishes right out of the pan!

the best vegan ribs

Serves: 2–3

These vegan ribs are a showstopper. I made these ribs for one of my closest, pickiest friends. She is someone that will tell you the real, really quickly. Not to my surprise, she absolutely loved these ribs! And for that reason, they are absolutely the meal to bring to any vegan skeptic because they are mind-blowingly flavorful and "meaty." I also strongly suggest this recipe to anyone struggling during a vegan transition.

1 tbsp (14 g) brown sugar

1 tsp onion powder

2 tsp (6 g) garlic powder

1 tsp mustard powder

½ tsp paprika

¼ tsp cayenne

¼ tsp smoked paprika

2 (14-oz [400-g]) cans jackfruit (in brine or water)

1 (12-oz [340-g]) package vegan ground beef

¼ cup (40 g) white onion, diced

2 tbsp (30 ml) vegan Worcestershire

1 tsp liquid smoke

¾ cup (180 ml) vegan BBQ sauce of choice

Preheat the oven to 375°F (190°C). Line a baking sheet with foil.

Add the brown sugar, onion powder, garlic powder, mustard powder, paprika, cayenne and smoked paprika to a small bowl; mix and set aside.

Drain and thoroughly rinse the jackfruit. Using your hands, squeeze any excess moisture from the jackfruit, remove the buds and discard. Add the jackfruit to a large bowl along with the vegan ground beef, onion, vegan Worcestershire, liquid smoke and the spice mixture. Using a wooden spoon, mix until well incorporated, then add to the foil-lined baking sheet and shape into a large rectangle. Using a butter knife, create four to five lines in the mixture, only slicing one quarter of the way through the mixture to create your rib shape.

Bake, uncovered, for 1 hour and 10 minutes. Remove from the oven and spread the BBQ sauce over the ribs. Return the pan to the oven and bake for another 20 minutes. Fully cut through the ribs along the lines you made in the mixture. Separate into ribs and serve.

smoky BBQ shredded jackfruit

 Serves: 2-3

Growing up, baked barbeque chicken was a huge staple in my home because it was so quick and easy to make. Now, for me to get that same feeling as a vegan, I make this delicious Smoky BBQ Shredded Jackfruit. If you have never had jackfruit before, you're in for a real treat; the texture is incredibly similar to that of shredded chicken breast! I use this recipe for loaded jackfruit sliders, pizzas and almost anywhere a good piece of chicken belongs.

1 (14-oz [400-g]) can jackfruit (in brine or water)

1 cup (240 ml) vegan BBQ sauce

¼ white or yellow onion, sliced

3–4 cloves garlic, finely chopped

1 tbsp (15 ml) avocado oil

1 tsp liquid smoke

1–2 tsp vegan grilled meat seasoning

½ tsp smoked paprika

Drain and rinse the jackfruit. Thoroughly shred the jackfruit and remove the seeded buds. Pat the jackfruit dry with a paper towel and place in a medium bowl. Add the BBQ sauce, onion, garlic, avocado oil, liquid smoke, grilled meat seasoning and smoked paprika. Mix well then add to a medium-sized saucepan over medium heat. Cook until fully heated through and the onion is tender, 10 to 12 minutes.

I recommend eating it on wheat slider buns with a bit of vegan coleslaw as pictured, or enjoy it in a wrap or bowl.

"ground beef" tempeh

Serves: 4

Ground beef was a staple in my home growing up—from tacos to pasta dishes—it was one of the most often used meats in my household (second to chicken of course). This vegan ground beef has the perfect texture and umami taste that we are all looking for in a good vegan ground beef. I love to use it for my taco nights!

1 (8-oz [226-g]) package tempeh

¼ cup (11 g) nutritional yeast

2 tbsp (30 ml) low sodium soy sauce or vegan Worcestershire

¼ cup (60 ml) chicken-less chicken stock/broth

1–2 tbsp (8–16 g) salt-free seasoning blend of choice

Smoked paprika, to taste

Salt and pepper, to taste

½ cup (75 g) chopped bell peppers

¼ cup (80 g) chopped red onion

2–3 cloves garlic, diced

2 tbsp (30 ml) avocado oil

Preheat the oven to 400°F (205°C). Line a baking pan with foil.

In a large bowl, break down the tempeh into medium/small chunks. Add the nutritional yeast, soy sauce or Worcestershire, stock, seasoning blend, smoked paprika, salt, pepper, bell peppers, onion and garlic and mix.

Spread the mixture on the foil-lined pan and drizzle with the avocado oil. Mix until well coated, then spread flat on the pan, leaving some space between each tempeh chunk. Bake for 30 minutes. Enjoy!

crowd's favorite tofu bacon

 Serves: 4

Everyone, and I mean everyone, loves this tofu bacon recipe. It's one of the top dishes I serve to vegan skeptics because it's absolutely delicious and tastes like the real thing. If you have a bacon obsession that you just can't seem to fight, you need to try this recipe.

¼ cup (60 ml) avocado oil

¼ cup (60 ml) low-sodium soy sauce, liquid aminos, coconut aminos or vegan Worcestershire

1 tbsp (15 ml) maple syrup

1 tsp liquid smoke

½ tsp garlic powder

½ tsp smoked paprika

½ tsp red chili flakes

Salt and pepper, to taste

7 oz (198 g) extra-firm tofu

Preheat the oven to 400°F (205°C).

In a medium bowl, combine the avocado oil, soy sauce, syrup, liquid smoke, garlic powder, paprika, chili flakes, salt and pepper and set aside.

Pat the tofu dry with a paper towel. Break the tofu into chunks, adding it to the marinade. Mix until fully combined.

Lay the tofu on a baking sheet and spread it evenly. Bake for 25 to 30 minutes, checking it periodically to make sure it does not burn.

Use as a topping on salads, beans or eat alone.

smoky pinto beans

 Serves: 4

This recipe is one of my favorites! It's what I typically make my partner on a weeknight when we need something quick that tastes like it's been cooking all day. I love to pair this with brown or jasmine rice and a plantain or two.

1 batch Crowd's Favorite Tofu Bacon (page 71)

2 (15.5-oz [439-g]) cans unsalted pinto beans

1–2 tbsp (30–45 ml) avocado oil

½ yellow onion

3 cloves garlic

1 cup (240 ml) vegetable broth or vegan chicken broth

¼ cup (60 ml) water

½ tbsp (8 ml) liquid smoke

Salt, to taste

While the Crowd's Favorite Tofu Bacon is in the oven, drain and rinse the beans.

Add the oil to a saucepan over medium–high heat and warm for about 2 minutes. Add the onion half and whole garlic cloves. Sauté until charred, 3 to 4 minutes. Add the beans, vegetable broth, water, liquid smoke and salt and reduce the heat to medium–low. Cook for about 10 minutes, stirring periodically. Then, using a large wooden spoon or potato masher, quickly mash the beans until you get your desired texture.

Top the beans with the Crowd's Favorite Tofu Bacon and enjoy.

go-to savory lentils

Cheap AND packed with nutrients, protein and flavor. Sign me up! These lentils literally will fill your home with fragrance; they are one of my favorite dishes to make when I want something homey and luscious. They are best served over mashed potatoes!

1 tbsp (15 ml) avocado oil

½ yellow onion, thickly sliced

3 cloves garlic

1 bay leaf

1 tsp basil

1 tsp garlic powder

Pepper, to taste

1 cup (192 g) raw lentils (not split)

2 cups (480 ml) vegetable broth or vegan chicken broth

1 tbsp (15 ml) soy sauce or vegan Worcestershire

1 cup (240 ml) water

Add the avocado oil to a medium pot and heat on medium heat for 1 to 2 minutes. Add the onion, garlic, bay leaf, basil, garlic powder and pepper and sauté until fragrant, about 3 minutes. Add the lentils and stir until well combined. Pour in the broth, soy sauce and water and bring to a medium boil. Boil for 3 minutes, then turn down the heat to low, cover and cook until tender, 20 to 25 minutes.

10-minute crispy tofu

Serves: 2–3

If you struggle to enjoy tofu due to its texture, this is the perfect beginner-friendly recipe for you: It's crispy on the outside and nice and tender on the inside. For those transitioning to adding tofu to their diet, I recommend using this tofu on a flavorful pasta dish or adding it to a wrap for a quick protein solution.

14 oz (397 g) extra-firm tofu

¼ cup (32 g) cornstarch

2 tbsp (30 ml) avocado oil

Drain and pat dry the tofu with a paper towel or a cloth. Dice or pull the tofu into large chunks. Add the tofu and cornstarch to a medium bowl and gently mix to lightly coat each piece.

In a large nonstick pan on medium–high heat, warm the oil then add the tofu and cook on one side until crispy, 3 to 5 minutes, then flip and cook for an additional 3 to 5 minutes, until crispy. Enjoy as a topping on your favorite dish.

spicy silken tofu

 Serves: 2

Year one of my vegan journey, you could not pay me to eat cold tofu out of a package. Fast forward to almost year three and I can't get enough! If you are experimenting with cold tofu, let this be your first go-round. It's packed with so much flavor and protein (secretly)! Not to mention you can whip this up in 10 minutes or less!

1 (14-oz [397-g]) package silken tofu

2 tbsp (30 ml) low-sodium soy sauce

2 tbsp (30 ml) rice wine vinegar

½ tbsp (8 ml) agave or organic sugar

1 tbsp (15 g) grated ginger

1 tbsp (15 ml) sriracha

2–3 cloves garlic, chopped

1 tbsp (8 g) sesame seeds (optional)

¼ cup (60 ml) water

1 green onion, diced

Drain the tofu and place on a serving plate.

In a medium bowl, stir together the soy sauce, vinegar, agave, ginger, sriracha, garlic, sesame seeds (if using) and water and mix until well incorporated. Add the mixture to a medium sauce-pan on low–medium heat along with the green onion and let the mixture heat through, 3 to 5 minutes. Top the tofu with the warmed mixture and enjoy.

soup, salads and sides!

Growing up, I loved a good side; as a vegan, life has only gotten better in the sides department. Within this chapter, there are a ton of monumental recipes that have shaped my pre-vegan life that I knew needed to be veganized. For instance, the Cabbage and Bacon (page 86) recipe is a carbon copy of my grandmother's simply delicious recipe, and the Southern-Style Greens (page 89) remind me of the smoky, salty, spicy greens my aunt would make. Truthfully, the list goes on in this section. It's filled with recipes that remind me of a time and place when food brought happiness, whether that be the sharing of food with others, or the intimate dish you make for yourself. I wish I could write a favorite call-out list, but the list would be the entire chapter. With that said, dig in!

vegan lasagna soup

 Serves: 4

If you are looking for a one-pot quick meal that will feed the whole family, this dish is your lifesaver! It's got the great taste of a lasagna but can be made in half the time and with less effort because, let's face it, who has time to make lasagna? I love to use lentils as my meat substitute in this dish because when they brew in the tomato sauce and broth they become so luscious! But, don't be afraid to sub your favorite vegan meatballs for the lentils. Enjoy!

1 tsp onion powder

1 tsp red chili flakes

1 tsp garlic powder

2 tsp (3 g) dried basil

1 tsp oregano

½ tsp paprika

½ tsp smoked paprika

Salt and pepper, to taste

1 bay leaf

16 oz (480 ml) pasta sauce

1 cup (192 g) raw lentils of choice or sub 6 oz (170 g) vegan meatballs

Large handful of kale

8 oz (226 g) cherry tomatoes

½ cup (120 ml) vegan cream (plant-based milk or cashew cream, optional)

8 oz (226 g) lasagna noodles, broken in half

In a small bowl, stir together the onion powder, chili flakes, garlic powder, basil, oregano, paprika, smoked paprika and salt and pepper. Add the bay leaf and set aside.

Add the pasta sauce to a large pot. Fill the empty pasta sauce container with water and add it to the pot. Do this a total of three times to equal 6 cups (1.4 L) of water. Next, add the seasoning mixture, lentils, kale, tomatoes and cream (if using).

Cook for 15 minutes on medium–low heat, then add the lasagna noodles. Cook for an additional 15 minutes.

Enjoy with friends and family!

creamy broccoli cheddar soup

 Serves: 4

No one forgets the first time they had broccoli cheddar soup. I remember in my pre-vegan life loving the cheesy goodness that kept me coming back! There is no secret broccoli cheddar soup recipe in our family, but let's be honest, Panera's version is everyone's staple. Making a vegan version that not only is packed with protein but also still reminds you of the goodness of the first bite of broccoli cheddar soup was essential. I hope this brings you back, as it does for me.

1 whole head garlic

3 cups (270 g) broccoli florets, divided, plus more for garnish (optional)

½ red bell pepper, deseeded

Salt and pepper, to taste

1 tbsp + 1 tsp (22 ml) avocado oil (or preferred oil), divided

1 cup (146 g) cashews

1 cup (200 g) dried chickpeas

2 cups (480 ml) vegan milk

½ cup (22 g) nutritional yeast

½ lemon, juiced

¼ cup (40 g) chopped onion

1 tsp garlic powder

1 tsp onion powder

½ tsp red chili flakes

Pumpkin seeds, for garnish

Bread, for serving

Preheat the oven to 375°F (190°C). Line a baking sheet with foil.

Slice off about one quarter of the top of the head of garlic and add it to the foil-lined baking sheet along with 1½ cups (135 g) of the broccoli florets and the red bell pepper. Top with some salt, pepper and about 1 tablespoon (15 ml) of the avocado oil. Bake for 25 minutes then remove the broccoli and red pepper and set aside. Return the pan with the garlic to the oven and bake 10 more minutes. When cool enough to handle, squeeze the garlic out of the paper husks and set aside.

While the vegetables are roasting, add the cashews and chickpeas to a pot of boiling water and boil for 15 to 20 minutes on a rapid boil. Drain.

In a separate pot of boiling water, boil the remaining 1½ cups (135 g) of broccoli florets until tender. Drain.

Add the boiled cashews and chickpeas, roasted garlic, roasted bell pepper, vegan milk, nutritional yeast and lemon juice to a blender and blend until lusciously smooth, then set aside.

Add 1 teaspoon of oil to a medium pot over medium heat. When warm, add the onion and sauté until tender, 3 to 5 minutes. Add the creamy sauce, the roasted broccoli, boiled broccoli, garlic powder, onion powder, chili flakes and 1 cup (240 ml) of water and mix. You can add more water for a thinner soup. Enjoy with an extra topping of roasted broccoli, pumpkin seeds and some bread!

cabbage and bacon

 Serves: 4

When I was growing up, my grandmother would make cabbage and bacon almost religiously. The slow cooker was her holy grail. I can still remember getting excited watching her make it. It seemed so simple, but no one can make it like her. This veganized version gets pretty close.

"bacon" bits

2 tbsp (30 ml) oil of choice

2 tbsp (30 ml) low-sodium soy sauce

2 tbsp (30 ml) vegan Worcestershire

1 tbsp (15 ml) maple syrup

½ tbsp (8 ml) liquid smoke

½ tsp garlic powder

½ tsp smoked paprika

½ tsp red chili flakes

½ tsp onion powder

Pepper, to taste

7 oz (198 g) extra-firm tofu

cabbage

½ head of a large cabbage

1 tbsp (15 ml) oil of choice

½ onion, thinly sliced

5 cloves garlic, diced

½ cup (120 ml) apple cider vinegar

⅓ cup (80 ml) maple syrup

1 tbsp (7 g) red chili flakes

2 bay leaves

Salt and pepper, to taste

1 cup (240 ml) vegetable stock/broth

To make the "Bacon" Bits, in a medium bowl, whisk the oil, soy sauce, vegan Worcestershire, maple syrup, liquid smoke, garlic powder, smoked paprika, chili flakes, onion powder and pepper. Add the tofu, toss to combine, then set aside.

Wash and chop the cabbage into thinly sliced strips. Add the oil to a large pot over medium heat then add the chopped cabbage, onion and garlic. Sauté for 5 minutes, then add the apple cider vinegar, maple syrup, red chili flakes, bay leaves, salt, pepper, vegetable stock and enough water to cover the ingredients, 4 to 6 cups (960 ml–1.4 L). Cook until tender, about 3 hours.

When the cabbage is a bit more than halfway through the cook time, preheat the oven to 400°F (205°C).

Add the "Bacon" Bits to a sheet pan and cook for 20 to 25 minutes.

When the cabbage is tender serve with the "Bacon" Bits on top.

southern-style greens

 Serves: 4-6

Every single Thanksgiving and Christmas you can find a pot of greens on the stove at my house. If you have ever had greens, you know that everyone makes it in their own special way. My grandmother oversimplified her greens, whereas my aunt always adds some meat and seasonings to hers for extra flair. One thing for sure, my greens had to leave an impact. Say hello to the greens that no one will know are vegan.

4–5 large bunches collard greens

2 tbsp (30 ml) oil of choice

1 white onion, roughly chopped

½ red onion, roughly chopped

1 whole jalapeño

5–10 cloves garlic, roughly chopped

¼ cup (60 ml) apple cider vinegar

½ cup (120 ml) Louisiana hot sauce

1 tbsp (15 ml) liquid smoke

2–3 (32-oz [946-ml]) cartons vegetable broth

1 tbsp (7 g) paprika

1 tbsp (7 g) onion powder

1 tbsp (15 g) sugar

1 tbsp (6 g) mustard powder

1 tbsp (8 g) garlic powder

Salt and pepper, to taste

Wash and chop the greens thoroughly.

Add the collards, oil, onion, jalapeño, garlic, apple cider vinegar, hot sauce, liquid smoke, vegetable broth, paprika, onion powder, sugar, mustard powder, garlic powder and salt and pepper to a giant pot over high heat. Bring to a boil for 5 minutes, and then a low simmer for 3 hours. Stir occasionally, but keep in mind that this is a low-lift recipe. Greens should be fork tender before serving.

pro tip: I like to prep this the night before without the vegetable broth. In the morning, add the broth and set it to simmer all day.

sweet and spicy wedges

 Serves: 2

These sweet potato wedges are the perfect fries fix! Growing up, there was a famous story of me enjoying KFC wedges so much that I once "snatched" a wedge from my mother's hands. Based on that story, I would say I know my wedges pretty well! These wedges are delicious, savory, spicy and sweet all at once.

1 sweet potato

3 tbsp (45 ml) oil of choice, divided

1 tbsp (3 g) nutritional yeast

½ tsp paprika

½ tsp garlic powder

¼ tsp cayenne

Salt and pepper, to taste

Preheat the oven to 400°F (205°C). Line a baking sheet with foil.

Wash, dry and cut the sweet potato into thick wedges.

Add the sweet potato wedges, 2 tablespoons (30 ml) of the oil, the nutritional yeast, paprika, garlic powder, cayenne and salt and pepper to a large bowl. Mix thoroughly and place flat on the foil-lined baking sheet, leaving ½ inch (1 cm) of space between the wedges. Drizzle with the remaining 1 tablespoon (15 ml) of oil.

Bake for 25 to 30 minutes.

Enjoy with my Zesty Cilantro Lime Sauce (page 111), or indulge however you like!

heart of palm ceviche

 Serves: 2–3

A few years back I came up with this recipe for my sister's graduation party. It was a hot summer day, and we needed something refreshing and light to eat as we prepared other dishes. Once my family tried this ceviche, it stuck as a BBQ tradition! It is the perfect dish to eat with some tortilla chips or on top of a toasted tostada with a cold refreshing drink to match. I hope you love this dish as much as my family does!

1 (15.5-oz [439-g]) can heart of palm

¼ cup (40 g) red onion, chopped

½ cup (75 g) green bell pepper, chopped

½ cup (75 g) red bell pepper, chopped

3–4 sheets of seaweed, chopped

1–2 tsp garlic powder

Salt and pepper, to taste

2 large lemons, juiced, including pulp (see Pro Tip)

2 large limes, juiced, including pulp (see Pro Tip)

Red chili flakes, for garnish

1 large avocado, sliced, for garnish (optional)

Drain the heart of palm and rinse thoroughly. Chop into medium–large chunks and add to a medium bowl. Add the onion, bell peppers, seaweed, garlic powder, salt and pepper. Top with the lemon and lime juice and pulp (omitting the seeds). Mix again and top with red chili flakes and avocado (if using). Adjust seasonings to your liking.

Refrigerate for 30 minutes to 1 hour, then serve.

pro tip: To add the pulp of the lemon and lime, after juicing, gently scoop out the flesh of the citrus using a spoon, being sure to remove any seeds.

refreshing cucumber tofu salad

Serves: 2–3

There comes a point in your vegan journey when you start to say, "Tofu isn't all that bad!" In fact, tofu is so versatile and it is perfect for just about any dish. Then you upgrade and realize that you can eat tofu straight from the package. Sounds frightening at first if you are not used to it, but I urge you to make this recipe your first go at a cold tofu dish! It is easy to make, flavorful and packed with protein. P.S., if you are on the search for a low-carb, high-protein meal, this is the dish for you!

3–4 baby cucumbers

11 oz (312 g) extra-firm tofu

¼ cup (60 ml) soy sauce

¼ cup (60 ml) rice wine vinegar

2–4 cloves garlic, minced

2 tsp (10 ml) agave

2 small green onions, minced

1 tbsp (15 g) minced fresh ginger

Red chili flakes, to preference (optional)

Wash and dice the cucumbers and tofu.

In a bowl, mix the soy sauce, rice wine vinegar, garlic, agave, onions and ginger until well combined. Add the red chili flakes to preference if you like it spicy (if using).

Top the tofu and cucumber with the sauce, mix and dig in. Feel free to marinate overnight in the fridge if desired.

green goddess salad

 Serves: 3–4

When I decided to join in the fun and create a vegan version of the viral Green Goddess dressing for my blog, I had no clue the recipe would go viral on its own and become one of my most viewed recipes to date! This dressing screams fresh, fragrant, flavorful. Not to mention it's packed with nutrients and protein. Top your favorite salad, wraps or veggie burgers with this dressing for an extra punch of pizzaz that will have you grabbing seconds.

green goddess dressing

1 cup (24 g) basil

½ cup (8 g) cilantro

1–3 fresh mint leaves

⅓ cup (53 g) hemp seeds

¼ cup (11 g) nutritional yeast

½ lemon, juiced

¼ cup (60 ml) avocado oil (or oil of choice)

2–3 cloves garlic

1 shallot

2–3 jalapeño slices

Pinch of salt

salad

3–4 baby cucumbers, diced

½ head cabbage, diced

3–4 green onions, diced

To make the Green Goddess Dressing, add the basil, cilantro, mint, hemp seeds, nutritional yeast, lemon juice, avocado oil, garlic, shallot, jalapeño, salt and ¼ cup (60 ml) of water to a blender and blend on high for 5 minutes until smooth. If you'd like a thinner dressing, add more water until you reach your desired consistency.

Store in an airtight container in the fridge for up to 3 days.

To make the salad, add the cucumbers, cabbage and green onions to a large bowl. Top the salad with the Green Goddess Dressing, mix and enjoy.

sauces
and creamy
cheeses

Probably the most important part of any vegan diet is flavor, and this chapter brings just that. I use each recipe in this section almost daily as a topping to a salad or wrap or even a creamy addition to a vegan cheese pizza. I have found that throughout my vegan journey, other people think that a vegan diet lacks nostalgia, flavor and texture. Within this section I prove that all wrong. Some highlights for me are the Herb-Infused "Feta" (page 119) and the Best-Ever Ranch Dressing (page 103). Plus, the Creamy Nacho "Cheese" (page 123) brings back all the joy of dipping into your favorite cheese sauce as a kid! It will be the star of your Super Bowl party or the perfect topping for your at-home nachos.

creamy dreamy cashew cream

 Serves: 6

Something that I truly missed as a vegan was the creaminess that dairy brought. As a child I loved mac and cheese, alfredo and ranch to dip my fries into! This recipe is an awesome base for just about any creamy sauce you desire. I specifically love to use it for my Creamy Alfredo (page 51). Just three simple ingredients, packed with healthy fat and protein.

1 cup (146 g) cashews of choice (raw or roasted unsalted)

¾ cup (180 ml) oat milk

Sprinkle of salt

Add 4 cups (960 ml) of water to a medium pot and bring to a rolling boil. Add the cashews and boil for 15 to 20 minutes, until tender. You may need to add more water to sustain the rolling boil. Drain and add your cashews to a blender along with the oat milk and salt and blend until smooth.

Store in an airtight container in the fridge for 1 week and enjoy in your favorite meals or as a sauce on its own.

Enjoy as a base for Creamy Alfredo as pictured on page 50, or as a topping to your favorite wraps and tacos.

best-ever ranch dressing

 Serves: 4

Cool ranch dressing on hot fries still gets me to this day. The creaminess of the ranch brings back memories from childhood. I was never the child to put ranch on my pizza (please forgive me), but I was an avid fry-ranch-dipper. Whether you pair this recipe with hot fries, your favorite salad or on top of your favorite vegan patty, this ranch is a crowd pleaser that will satisfy anyone. Did I mention there are 20 grams of protein in each batch?

½ cup (120 ml) vegan milk

1 tbsp (15 ml) apple cider vinegar

¾ cup (180 ml) vegan mayo (can sub with unsweetened vegan yogurt)

6 tbsp (60 g) hemp seeds

2 cloves garlic

½ lemon, juiced

¼ tsp onion powder

Salt and pepper, to taste

2–4 stalks fresh chives, chopped

Dill, chopped, to taste

In a small cup, stir together the vegan milk and apple cider vinegar and let sit 2 to 5 minutes to thicken and form vegan buttermilk.

Add the vegan buttermilk mixture, mayo, hemp seeds, garlic, lemon juice, onion powder, salt and pepper to a blender. Blend for 5 minutes, until smooth. If you prefer thinner ranch, add 2 tablespoons (30 ml) of water at a time and then blend, until you get your desired texture.

Gently fold the chopped chives and dill into the mixture. Taste the mixture and adjust the dill to your preference.

Store in the fridge in an airtight container for up to 1 week.

go-to tahini dressing

Serves: 2

Believe it or not, I used to have no clue what the heck tahini was or what it was made from. If this is your first time hearing of tahini, let me give you a breakdown: It's a nut butter made from sesame seeds that has a bitter, nutty flavor that pairs perfectly with a touch of acid. It is also rich in antioxidants and high in plant-based protein! Tahini pairs perfectly with salads and Mediterranean-style dishes. I have grown to love tahini and, with this recipe, I know you will, too!

2 tbsp (30 ml) tahini

½ lemon, juice and pulp (see Pro Tip)

2 cloves garlic, minced

1 tbsp (15 ml) oil of choice

1–2 tsp (4–8 ml) maple syrup

Salt and pepper, to taste

Combine the tahini, lemon juice and pulp, garlic, oil, maple syrup and salt and pepper to a small bowl. Mix well then add 1 to 2 tablespoons (15–30 ml) of water at a time until you find the consistency you prefer. Pour over a salad or bowl of choice.

pro tip: To add the pulp of the lemon, after juicing, gently scoop out the flesh of the citrus using a spoon, being sure to remove any seeds.

spicy ginger turmeric dressing

 Serves: 1

Turmeric is probably one of my favorite spices of all the spices in the world! Why? Well, I'm glad you asked! Turmeric has an agent call curcumin, which is known to improve heart health and prevent Alzheimer's disease and cancer. Preventing cancer is so important to me because it runs in my family. The curcumin can be activated in turmeric when you add a little pepper. Let's not forget that the turmeric adds a beautiful color and earthy balance to almost any sauce or meal. You will love how much color this sauce brings to your plate, not to mention how much flavor!

2 cloves garlic

½ tsp minced fresh ginger

2 tbsp (30 ml) tahini

1 tbsp (15 ml) hemp oil (or oil of choice)

1 tbsp (15 ml) organic maple syrup

½ tsp turmeric powder

½ tsp mustard powder

1–2 tsp red chili flakes

Salt and pepper, to taste

Finely chop the garlic and place it in a small bowl. Add the ginger, tahini, hemp oil, maple syrup, turmeric, mustard powder, red chili flakes and salt and pepper and stir to combine. Add 1 to 2 tablespoons (15–30 ml) of water at a time and mix until you achieve the desired texture.

Serve this over your favorite salad or bowl, or use as a dip for fries!

Store in the fridge for up to 4 days.

super greens guacamole

Serves: 4

Now, I love me some guac. That's it.

Just kidding! This is a cookbook, after all. I have to say, guac has a special place in my heart. Growing up in California, I can think of countless girls' nights when we all laughed and shared stories over a platter of guac and crispy tortilla chips. Of course, I had to step it up and make a protein-packed version that brings Taco Tuesday to a whole new level. This recipe is packed with 11 grams of plant-based protein thanks to our friend edamame.

1½ large avocados or 2–3 small avocados

½ cup (46 g) edamame, fresh or frozen

¼ red onion, diced

½ Roma tomato, diced

¼ red bell pepper, diced

¼ green bell pepper, diced

1 tbsp (5 g) chopped jalapeño

½ lemon, juiced (include pulp; see Pro Tip)

1 lime, juiced (include pulp; see Pro Tip)

Handful cilantro, diced

½–1 tsp garlic powder

½ tsp onion powder

1 tsp red chili flakes

Salt and pepper, to taste

Slice the avocados in half and gently press the back shell until you can remove the seed. Using a spoon, remove the smooth flesh of the avocados and place it in a medium bowl, then mash.

Prepare the edamame according to package directions if frozen.

Add the edamame to the avocados and mash until you achieve a smooth, yet slightly chunky, consistency. Add the red onion, tomato, bell peppers, jalapeño, lemon and lime juice and pulp, cilantro, garlic powder, onion powder, chili flakes and salt and pepper and mix well.

Enjoy in a bowl, on a taco or simply with some chips while chatting with the girls (or guys!).

pro tip: To add the pulp of the lemon and lime, after juicing, gently scoop out the flesh of the citrus using a spoon, being sure to remove any seeds.

zesty cilantro lime sauce

Serves: 2

The star of this sauce is the creamy texture, all thanks to hemp seeds, which are protein-packed, full of healthy fat and my literal obsession. The cilantro and lime are the most refreshing combination and make this sauce a triple threat: creamy, zesty and rich in protein. This sauce is perfect for topping any wrap or for dipping with my Sweet and Spicy Wedges (page 90).

3 tbsp (30 g) hemp seeds or hearts

3–4 tbsp (45–60 ml) vegan milk of choice (see Pro Tip), divided

Pinch salt

2–3 tbsp (2–3 g) cilantro

1 lime, juiced

Add the hemp seeds, 3 tablespoons (45 ml) of the vegan milk, salt, cilantro and lime juice to a blender. Blend until smooth, 1 to 3 minutes. Check the texture and add the remaining 1 tablespoon (15 ml) of vegan milk if you desire a thinner consistency.

pro tip: The type of milk you choose will impact the texture. For creamier sauce add creamier milks (e.g., cashew); for thinner sauce, go with almond.

spicy peanut butter sauce

 Serves: 2

This Spicy Peanut Butter Sauce is the perfect marinade for any tofu you have laying around that needs a flavor blast! Or, if you are craving an Asian-style tofu and veg plate, this is the perfect topping. This sauce reminds me of all the times in college I would sneak away to the student union to splurge at our very own Panda Express on campus. This sauce is a reflection of those old cravings in a heathier package that has matured as much as I have. Packed with healthy fat from peanuts and jammed with antioxidants from ginger, say hello to your newest weekly obsession.

2 tbsp (32 g) peanut butter or peanut butter powder

¼ cup (60 ml) low-sodium soy sauce

1–2 tbsp (6–12 g) pre-minced ginger

2–3 tsp (10–15 ml) sriracha

Add the peanut butter, soy sauce, ginger and sriracha to a medium bowl and mix until smooth. Add water to thin it out, 1 tablespoon (15 ml) at a time, until you get your desired texture.

Use as an overnight marinade for tofu or pour over your stir-fry for an extra kick!

best-ever hummus

 Serves: 4

When I figured out you can make hummus at home, it was game over. I am a hummus fanatic and you will likely find a tub of this stuff in my fridge year-round. The best part about this recipe is it stores perfectly up to a week in an airtight container (although you won't need to store it that long!) and it is 10x smoother than store-bought because of a trick I explain in the directions. Let's not forget chickpeas are a great source of carbs and extra protein. I love to use this hummus as a dip for some fresh baby cucumbers or inside of a lentil wrap!

1 (15.5-oz [439-g]) can chickpeas, drained

½ tsp baking soda

4–5 cloves garlic

½ cup (120 ml) fresh lemon juice (include pulp; see Pro Tip)

1 tsp cumin, divided

½ cup (120 ml) tahini

1 tbsp (15 ml) olive oil, plus more for drizzling

½ tsp garlic powder

1¼ –1½ tsp (8–9 g) fresh sea salt

Large pinch of cayenne

Paprika, for garnish

Flaky salt, for garnish

Fresh parsley, for garnish

Add the chickpeas, baking soda and garlic cloves to a pot of water and boil for 15 minutes on high. Adding the baking soda will make your chickpeas more tender, so do not skip it!

Drain and rinse the chickpeas and garlic cloves and add them to a food processor with the lemon juice and pulp, ½ teaspoon of the cumin and the tahini. Blend until smooth, 3 to 5 minutes. Add the olive oil, garlic powder, salt and cayenne and blend again. Pour into a bowl or airtight container and top with a drizzle of olive oil, the remaining ½ teaspoon of the cumin, a sprinkle of paprika, flaky salt and parsley!

pro tip: To add the pulp of the lemon, after juicing, gently scoop out the flesh of the citrus using a spoon, being sure to remove any seeds.

superfood "parm" crumbles

Serves: 4–6

This vegan "Parmesan" is packed with nutrients, healthy fats and protein. It's also easy to assemble and quite literally addicting! Add it to anything you desire—I love to use it to top my Spicy Lentil Bolognese (page 52) but feel free to add it to just about anything.

½ cup (73 g) raw cashews

¼ cup (11 g) nutritional yeast

¼ cup (40 g) hemp seeds

1 tsp onion powder

½ tsp dried basil

Sprinkle of salt

Add the cashews, nutritional yeast, hemp seeds, onion powder, basil and salt to a food processor and gently pulse until all ingredients are combined, 3 to 5 minutes. Be sure to carefully pulse to ensure your mixture doesn't become nut butter!

Store in an airtight container for 2 weeks. These crumbles do not need to be refrigerated.

herb-infused "feta"

 Serves: 3

I love this recipe; it's just so good. Believe it or not, "feta" is a highly requested recipe on my blog that I have been saving for this book because it's that special. Feta is one of those cold, refreshing cheeses that you can put on just about anything, and this vegan feta is no exception. It's the perfect addition to almost any salad or pizza.

2 tsp (11 g) miso paste

¼ cup (60 ml) lemon juice

¼ cup (60 ml) olive oil

1–2 tbsp (3–6 g) nutritional yeast

2 cloves garlic, minced

1 tsp garlic powder

½ tsp onion powder

1 tbsp (2 g) dried thyme

Salt and pepper, to taste

7 oz (198 g) extra-firm tofu

Add the miso, lemon juice, olive oil, nutritional yeast, minced garlic, garlic powder, onion powder, thyme, salt and pepper to a small bowl. Whisk until well combined.

Wrap the tofu in paper towels and gently press to remove excess liquid. Cube the tofu or cut into desired shapes. Add the tofu to the bowl with the marinade and toss to combine until well mixed. Add to an airtight container and refrigerate for 30 minutes, then serve.

Store in the fridge for up to 3 days.

tofu "ricotta"

Serves: 4

This recipe will knock your socks off because it is so creamy and delicious. So, basically everything "they" told you about vegan cheese wasn't true. This "ricotta" is made from protein-packed tofu. It is super easy to whip this up and add to the fridge until you are ready to indulge! Use this to top pizzas or pastas, or dig right in with some crackers.

1 (14-oz [397-g]) package extra-firm tofu

2 tbsp (6 g) nutritional yeast

½ tbsp (9 g) miso paste

½ fresh lemon, juiced

1½ tsp (4 g) garlic powder or 2 cloves garlic

1 tsp onion powder

2 tbsp (30 ml) olive oil or grapeseed oil

1 tsp coconut oil

Salt and pepper, to taste

1–2 basil leaves thinly chopped

Wrap the tofu in paper towels and gently press to remove excess moisture.

Add the tofu, nutritional yeast, miso, lemon juice, garlic powder, onion powder, olive oil, coconut oil and salt and pepper to a high-speed blender or food processor. Pulse five to eight times, for 15 seconds or less each time, until the mixture is nice and creamy but with a little texture.

Stir in the chopped basil and serve immediately, or store in the fridge for up to 3 days.

creamy nacho "cheese"

 Serves: 4

Super easy + super delicious! Not to mention it is made from cashews, which makes this "cheese" vegan, unbelievably creamy and packed with fat and protein. Did you know that incorporating cashews into your diet can promote weight loss, blood sugar control and heart health? I mean, when it tastes this good, why wouldn't you?

1 cup (146 g) raw, unsalted cashews

¾ cup (33 g) nutritional yeast

1 tsp onion powder

1 tsp turmeric

2 tsp (4 g) garlic powder

½ tsp chili powder

½ tsp paprika

1 cup (240 ml) unsweetened vegan milk

Salt and pepper, to taste

Add the cashews to a medium pot and fill with water. Bring the water to a boil and when it reaches a rolling boil, cook for 15 to 20 minutes, until the cashews are tender.

Drain the cashews and add them to a blender along with the nutritional yeast, onion powder, turmeric, garlic powder, chili powder, paprika, vegan milk, salt, pepper and ½ cup (120 ml) of water. Blend until nice and creamy, about 5 minutes.

Add the mixture to a pot over medium–low heat and stir to warm. If you would like, add water until you get your desired consistency—I add about ¼ cup (60 ml) of water.

easiest charcuterie board ever

 Serves: 4

In college I was the ringleader of every wine night. I was the one who would wrangle all my girls over to my home for a girls' night and this is a dish I knew would be the perfect quick fix. If you are looking for an easy crowd favorite that is secretly super easy to make, this is the recipe for you!

¼ cup (25 g) pecans or walnuts

2–3 dill sprigs

¼ cup (28 g) dried cranberries

1 lb (454 g) vegan cream cheese

Crackers, for serving

Grapes, for serving

Dried fruit, for serving

Vegan dark chocolate, for serving

Nuts of choice, for serving

Plant-based salami, for serving

Chop the pecans or walnuts into small/medium-sized bites.

Line a medium-sized bowl with plastic wrap and make sure it extends far enough on either side of the bowl to be able to cover the bowl. Add the dill to the bowl, then the nuts and dried cranberries. Top with the vegan cream cheese. Use the excess plastic wrap to cover the cheese, then place the bowl in the fridge for 30 minutes to set.

Unwrap the cheese and turn upside down on a charcuterie board. Enjoy with crackers, grapes, dried fruit, dark chocolate, nuts and plant-based salami.

dessert for the sweet toothed

What was your favorite dessert as a kid? Mine was cheese-cake, hands down! Seriously, I would ask for cheesecake as my birthday cake, that's how deep my love was. I now have an awesome vegan version that gives me all the same feels—see the Dreamy Cheesecake recipe (page 136). As another fun fact, a milkshake was one of the first recipes I can remember writing down as a child. It was called "The Ultimate Milkshake" to be exact, and truly I had heart for it. In this chapter, you can find my current version of the ulti-mate milkshake with my Creamy Nice Cream (page 140). We also can't forget that coffee ice cream was my mother's absolute favorite, so I had to make a veganized version (Easy Coffee Ice Cream on page 139). This just might be my favorite chapter in the book, but don't tell the others!

P.S., I won't judge if you come back for seconds.

cozy caramel

 Serves: 3–4

Vegan caramel! I loved caramel as a kid. I was never really a chocolate lover, but I was always a caramel lover. Becoming vegan and having my prized dessert stripped away from me left me feeling lost. I mean, I have a major sweet tooth! Creating this recipe gave me all the feelings of childhood without the milk, butter or sticky texture of traditional caramel. Enjoy this as a drizzle over your favorite ice cream, or add to the bottom of your coffee for a caramel drizzle!

1 cup (160 g) pitted dates

1 tsp vanilla

½ tsp caramel extract

¾–1 cup (180–240 ml) vegan milk of choice

Pinch of salt

Add the dates to a bowl and cover with boiling water. Let sit for 30 minutes to allow the dates to become tender.

Drain the dates and add them to a high-speed blender with the vanilla, caramel extract, vegan milk and salt and blend until smooth.

Pour into an airtight container and store for up to 3 days in the fridge.

vegan twix bars

Serves: 3–4

Because I'm obsessed with caramel, you can probably understand how I feel about Twix® bars, right? I mean, that was my candy growing up. Re-creating this cookie, caramel and chocolate bar has been a highlight of my career mostly because I not only made a delicious dessert but a nutritious dessert. Trust me, you will love these bars as much as I do.

1 (15.5-oz (439-g]) can salt-free chickpeas, drained

½ cup (120 ml) tahini

⅓ cup (80 ml) agave or maple syrup

1–2 tsp (5–10 ml) vanilla

½ tsp baking powder

½ tsp baking soda

Salt, to taste

1 batch Cozy Caramel (page 128)

1 cup (240 g) vegan dark chocolate chips

1–2 tsp (5–10 ml) coconut oil

Flaky salt, for sprinkling

Preheat the oven to 350°F (175°C). Line a 9 x 9–inch (23 x 23–cm) baking pan with parchment paper, then lightly oil it with your oil of choice.

To make the cookies, add the chickpeas, tahini, agave, vanilla, baking powder, baking soda and salt to a food processor and blend until smooth with no clumps, about 4 minutes.

Pour the mixture into the prepared baking pan and spread it out so it fills the pan. Bake for 18 to 20 minutes, until a toothpick inserted in the center comes out clean.

Put the pan in the fridge to let the cookie cool for 5 to 10 minutes.

Spread ½ to ¾ cup (120–180 ml) of the Cozy Caramel on top of the cookie and return the pan to the fridge for 30 minutes.

Remove the cookie from the fridge and cut horizontally, then vertically to make bars.

Add the chocolate and coconut oil to a microwave-safe dish and microwave in 30-second increments (mixing until smooth each time). Drizzle on top of the bars until all are completely covered, then top with flaky salt.

Put the bars in the freezer for 10 minutes until the chocolate is set, then enjoy!

edible cookie dough

 Serves: 4

This edible cookie dough is simply addicting! We all know eating cookie dough out of the package is a big no-no, but this cookie dough will keep your fueled and satisfied. It's made from chickpeas, which doesn't sound dessert-friendly, but I promise I would never steer you wrong. It's so good that I store it in my fridge for whenever I get a sweet tooth craving. This is the dessert to fool any vegan skeptic—be sure to tell them what's in it after they tell you how delicious it is.

1 (15.5-oz [439-g]) can chickpeas

¼ cup (60 ml) tahini

1 tbsp (16 g) peanut butter

3 tbsp (42 g) brown sugar

3 tbsp (45 ml) maple syrup

¼ cup + 1 tbsp (128 g) oat flour

2 tsp (10 ml) vanilla

Pinch of salt

½–1 cup (120–240 g) vegan dark chocolate chips

Line a cookie sheet with parchment paper. Set aside.

Drain, rinse and dry the chickpeas with a paper towel. Add the chickpeas, tahini, peanut butter, brown sugar, maple syrup, oat flour, vanilla and salt to a food processor and process for 5 minutes, until smooth.

Put the mixture in a medium bowl and chill in the fridge for 10 minutes.

Add ½ cup (120 g) of the chocolate chips if you're a conservative chocolate lover or the full 1 cup (240 g) if you're a true chocolate lover. Fold the chips into the dough until well combined, then chill in the fridge for 15 minutes.

Using a cookie scoop, scoop the dough onto the parchment-lined cookie sheet and place in the freezer for 5 minutes. Enjoy immediately, or store the dough balls in an airtight container in the fridge for up to 3 days.

decadent chocolate chip cookies

 Serves: 4

Say hello to the moistest cookie you have ever had in your life! The dough is so easy to whip up and is packed with protein. On top of that, these cookies are made with whole ingredients that will leave you feeling better after eating them. Now name another cookie that can do that!

1 (15.5-oz [439-g]) can chickpeas

¼ cup (60 ml) tahini

1 tbsp (16 g) peanut butter

3 tbsp (42 g) brown sugar

3 tbsp (45 ml) maple syrup

¼ cup + 1 tbsp (128 g) oat flour

2 tsp (10 ml) vanilla

Pinch of salt

1 tsp baking soda

½–¾ cup (120–180 g) vegan chocolate chips

Preheat the oven to 350°F (175°C).

Drain, rinse and dry the chickpeas with a paper towel. Add the chickpeas, tahini, peanut butter, brown sugar, maple syrup, oat flour, vanilla, salt and baking soda to a food processor. Pulse until you get a smooth dough, 4 to 5 minutes, then put the mixture in a medium bowl and chill in the fridge for 10 minutes to firm up the dough.

Add ½ cup (120 g) of the chocolate chips if you're a conservative chocolate lover or the full ¾ cup (180 g) if you're a true chocolate lover. Fold the chips into the dough until well combined, then place the batter back in the fridge for 10 minutes.

Using a cookie scoop, scoop the dough onto a cookie sheet and freeze for 10 minutes.

Place the cookie sheet in the oven and bake for 15 minutes. Remove the sheet from the oven and use a spatula to gently press the cookies to flatten. Allow the cookies to cool for 5 minutes.

Store in an airtight container for up to 4 days.

dreamy cheesecake

 Serves: 4

When I was a kid and you asked me what I wanted as my birthday cake I would say, "cheesecake!" I love cheesecake so much and being vegan doesn't have to stop my love affair. If there is anything that must make it into this cookbook, it's a delicious cheesecake. Let's not forget it's made from cashews, which create such a creamy rich texture that just so happens to be packed with protein and healthy fats.

2 cups (292 g) raw cashews

1 (13.5-oz [398-ml]) can full-fat coconut milk

⅔ cup (132 g) organic sugar or 4–5 dates

1 tbsp (15 ml) vanilla

1 lemon, juice and pulp (see Pro Tip)

1 lime, zest, juice and pulp (see Pro Tip)

Pinch of salt

1 (9-inch [23-cm]) pre-made vegan graham cracker crust

Fresh strawberries (optional), for garnish

Add the cashews to a pot of boiling water and cook for 15 to 20 minutes, until tender.

Drain the cashews and add them to a high-speed blender with the coconut milk, sugar (or dates), vanilla, lemon juice and pulp, lime zest, lime juice and pulp and salt. Blend to a smooth consistency, 3 to 5 minutes. If you are not using a high-speed blender, continue to blend for 9 to 15 minutes until you get a very smooth consistency.

Pour the mixture into the graham cracker crust then place in the freezer for at least 5 hours. When you are ready to serve, allow the cheesecake to thaw for at least 30 minutes before you dig in.

Decorate with fresh strawberries if you'd like.

Store leftovers in the fridge for up to 2 days; remember to return the cheesecake to the fridge after slicing!

pro tip: To add the pulp of the lemon and lime, after juicing, gently scoop out the flesh of the citrus using a spoon, being sure to remove any seeds.

easy coffee ice cream

 2–3

My mom's favorite ice cream when I was growing up was coffee, hence my favorite ice cream flavor was coffee. Turns out coffee ice cream isn't popular as a vegan flavor in the store, but luckily for you (and me) you can make it at home with this simple, fuss-free recipe.

1 cup (146 g) cashews

1 cup (120 g) dates

1 cup (240 ml) coffee

1 (13.5-oz [398-ml]) can full-fat coconut milk

1–2 tsp (5–10 ml) lemon juice or apple cider vinegar

1 tsp vanilla

Salt, to taste

Cinnamon, to taste

2 tbsp (30 ml) vegan milk of choice

Add 4 to 6 cups (960 ml–1.4 L) of water to a medium-sized pot over medium–high heat. Add the cashews and dates and boil for 15 minutes. Once tender, drain, then add the cashews, dates, coffee, coconut milk, lemon juice or vinegar, vanilla, salt and cinnamon to a high-speed blender and blend until smooth, approximately 5 minutes.

Pour the mixture into ice-cube trays (you may need two trays) and freeze overnight.

When the cubes are completely frozen, add them to a high-speed blender along with the vegan milk and blend until you get the consistency you would like. Serve immediately.

creamy nice cream

 Serves: 4

Ice cream that can be made at home and is healthy, creamy and delicious? Yes, please! This "nice cream" is so easy to make and is perfect for those nights you want a sweet treat that can be quickly made (and eaten). Be sure to freeze the bananas ahead of time! This recipe reminds me of the soft serve I would have at Fosters Freeze as a kid, and I promise this will bring the kid out in you!

4–5 large bananas

¼ cup (60 ml) coconut milk or cream

2 tbsp (30 ml) maple syrup

1 tbsp (15 ml) vanilla

Pinch of cinnamon

Pinch of salt

Toppings of choice

Peel the bananas, cut them in half, place them in a plastic bag and freeze overnight.

Add the frozen bananas, coconut milk, maple syrup, vanilla, cinnamon and salt to a high-speed blender. Blend until creamy, 2 to 5 minutes depending on blender size. Serve with your desired toppings.

Can be kept in the freezer for up to 5 days.

lemon sorbet

 Serves: 4

This recipe is the perfect palate cleanser! Eat it right after dinner to reset your body for the next day. It is so refreshing and tart! Did I mention this is low-calorie?

5–6 lemons

½ cup (120 ml) full-fat coconut milk

2 tbsp (30 g) organic sugar

1 tbsp (15 ml) vanilla

Peel the lemons and freeze them overnight, or until frozen solid.

Add the frozen lemons, coconut milk, sugar and vanilla to a blender. Blend until perfectly smooth, then serve!

Store in an airtight container in the freezer for up to 2 weeks.

orange sherbet

Serves: 4

Growing up we ate orange sherbet constantly (believe it or not). This sherbet is creamy, vanilla-y and has the perfect amount of orange. Plus, it is 10x better than any pre-made stuff at the store!

4–5 organic oranges

½ cup (120 ml) organic coconut cream

2 tbsp (30 ml) organic maple syrup

Pinch of salt

Cut the skin off the oranges and place them in the freezer overnight.

Add the oranges to a high-speed blender along with the coconut cream, maple syrup and salt. Blend until creamy, about 3 minutes, then enjoy!

Store in an airtight container in the freezer for up to 2 weeks.

about the author

Emani Marie Corcran is a vegan recipe and lifestyle content creator who caters to all people curious about expanding into the vegan lifestyle. She focuses on health and nutrition as a focal point in her creations, while crafting delicious meals that will entice even the most notorious meat eater.

She believes in inspiring her audience through action and sharing health and wellness tips along the way. Her goal is to bring vegan food into the cultural conversation as a means to give veganism a fresh, modern and flavorful turn from its previous past. She has a passion for curating a warm and welcoming environment that makes her page inclusive to everyone while explaining veganism from her African American perspective.

Emani Corcran is otherwise known as @blkandvegan.

acknowledgments

Thank you to Marissa, Meg and the entire Page Street team for believing in me and working with me! Thank you to my partner in crime, Fabio, for assisting me and holding my hand during this time. Thank you to Monika Normand for taking the most beautiful photographs of my food. Thank you to my family for being a constant inspiration to my recipes and a constant source of motivation. Lastly, thank you to every single person who follows and supports Blk and Vegan. Without you all, this book would not be a reality! I love you all and you each have a special place in my heart. To many more!

index